Home/Sch CONNECTIONS

Newbridge Discovery Links®—Early Level

Home/School Connections
Early Level
ISBN: 1-56784-081-7

Edited and Designed by Curriculum Concepts

Newbridge Educational Publishing
333 East 38th Street, New York, NY 10016

10 9 8 7 6 5 4 3

■ ■ ■ ■ ■ ■ ■ ■ ■ ■

Dear Teacher,

The Discovery Links program has been designed to support the development of children's reading skills and strategies while building and encouraging their natural curiosity about the world. These mini-books are easy to reproduce, and with supervision, children can assemble the books on their own to share their growth and learning in reading and science with family and friends.

The purpose of these reproducible mini-books is to extend the learning experience beyond the classroom by making it possible for every child to take a book home. Children are encouraged to take the books home and share knowledge they've discovered about their world. The books themselves are an excellent way for families to see a child's reading development as they move from simple caption books to longer and more complex texts.

The books in the Discovery Links program feature a strong text-to-photo match, repetitive language, and language patterns to help children learn and grow as readers. Children are invited to read about birds, archaeology, buildings, light, snails, corn, animals, the senses, recycling, the stars, and other high-interest science themes. With a solid foundation in the life, physical, and earth sciences, these books will help launch explorations, experiments, writing activities, art projects, and much more. And since these books are reproducible, children can read, refer to, and take the books along as they experiment, observe, write, and paint.

We hope you find useful ways to incorporate these reproducible mini-books into your reading and science studies. We believe the books are not only an effective teaching tool, but a wonderful home/school connection.

Happy Reading!

Brenda Parkes

Dr. Brenda Parkes
Early Literacy Specialist

■ ■ ■ ■ ■ ■ ■ ■ ■ ■

Early Level

Set A

Animals From Long Ago	Kittens
Animal Messengers	Let's Make Something New
At the Playground	Rocks
Beaks	Snails in School!
Bikes	Up Close
City Buildings	What Can Change?
Day and Night	What Does a Garden Need?
How Animals Move	Where Are the Eggs?

Set B

Animals Build	Our Senses
At the Science Center	Recycle It!
The Coral Reef	Sounds All Around
Corn: From Farm to Table	Stars
From the Earth	Taking Care of Baby
Fur, Feathers, Scales, Skin	Watching the Weather
Let's Bake	What Do Scientists Do?
Light and Shadow	Where Does the Water Go?

Assembly Instructions

Step 1

Make double-sided copies of the pages.

Step 2

Cut the pages in half along the dotted line and place the halves over each other.

Step 3

Place the pages together and fold.

Step 4

Staple the pages together.

Set A

There are no dinosaurs now.

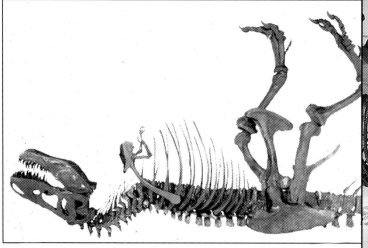

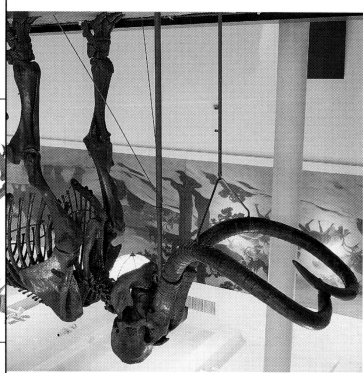

These are the bones of a mammoth.

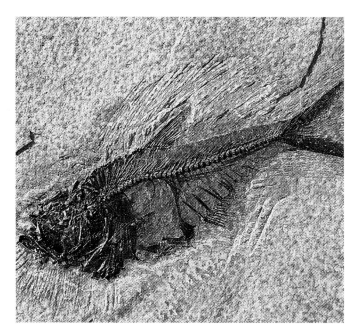

Here is another animal
from long ago.
What does it look like?

Animals From Long Ago

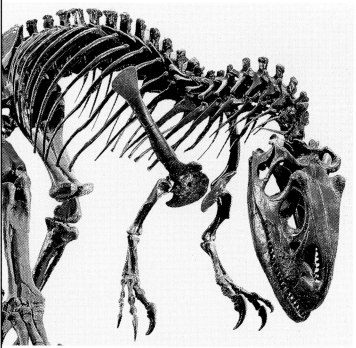

Christine Economos

People have found their old bones.
Prints and bones help us learn about these animals.

This painting shows what a big dinosaur looked like.

Long ago, there were animals we don't see today.
People have found their prints.

Today there are birds.
Birds have feet like dinosaurs.

There are no mammoths now.

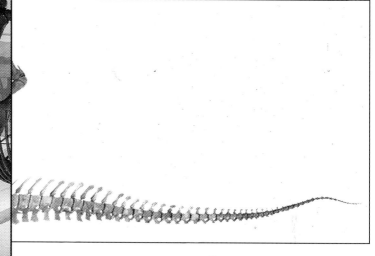

These are the bones of a big dinosaur.

These are the bones
of a saber-toothed cat.

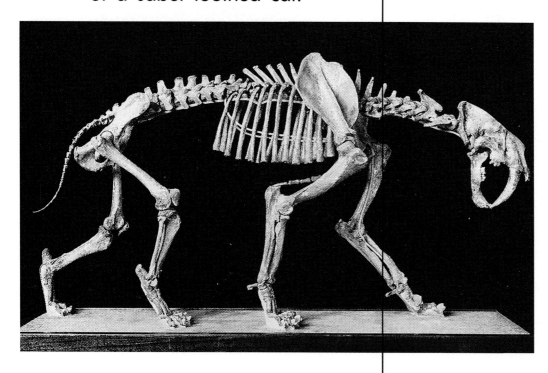

There are no
saber-toothed
cats now.

Today there are tigers.
They look like saber-toothed cats
in some ways.

This painting shows what
mammoths looked like.

This painting shows what a
saber-toothed cat looked like.

Today there are elephants.
They look like mammoths
in some ways.

These prairie dogs touch noses. This touch means, "Hello!"

People have many ways to send messages.

Index

Animal
Messengers

Brenda Parkes

People can write.

My cat is telling me something.

People can talk.

I get the message!
It's time for her to eat.

Some animals send messages by touching.

Some animals use signals
to send messages.
This bird signals, "Look at me!"

This deer flashes
its white tail.
This signal means,
"Danger!"

Animals are different.
Some animals send
messages by making sounds.

A scientist made this diagram
to show how the bee dances.

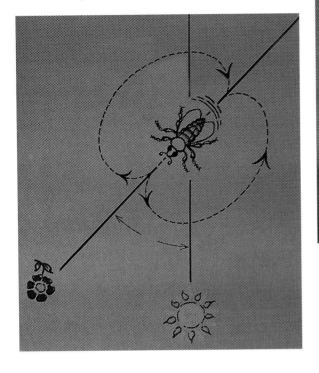

This bee is doing a dance.
This signal means,
"I know where to find food!"

This snake shakes the rattle
on its tail.
The sound means, "Watch out!"

I scoop it up with a pail.
I make a big hill.

I like to go on the slide.
I climb up, up, up.

How can we climb this?

At the
Playground

Christine Economos

Come and see what we can do.

We like to climb.
We pull ourselves up.

Come to the playground.

We use our hands, arms,
and legs to climb to the top.

I slide
down, down, down.

I like to play in the sand.
I push the sand with my hands.

We like the balance beam.
We put one foot
in front of the other.

I like to go in the tunnel.
I curl up to fit inside.

The swing goes
higher and higher.
It feels like flying.

I like the merry-go-round.
I run and push.

I like the swing.
I pump with my legs
to go back and forth.

We hold on to the bars.
The merry-go-round spins around.

They use their beaks
to find food in the soft mud.

How is this bird
using its beak?

This is a parrot.
Parrots have short, sharp beaks.

Beaks

Brenda Parkes

A bird's beak helps it
get food and eat it.

This is a toucan.
Look at its big, long beak!

Birds have beaks.

Toucans use their beaks
to help them reach fruit.

They use their beaks
to open hard nuts.

This is a flamingo.
Flamingos have big, curved beaks.

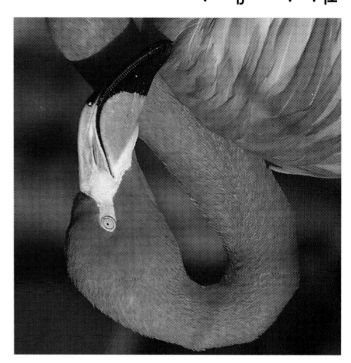

This is a hummingbird.
Hummingbirds have long, thin beaks.

They use their beaks
to sip nectar from flowers.

They use their beaks
to catch fish.

This is a robin.
Robins have small, pointed beaks.

These are puffins.
Puffins have small, curved beaks.

They use their beaks
to catch worms.

If a bike has a flat tire,
the bike won't go!

Bikes have wheels.

Parts of a Bike

handlebars ······

seat ···

tire

pedal

wheel

Every bike has many parts.
How many parts can you name?

Bikes

Daniel Jacobs

Big people ride big bikes.

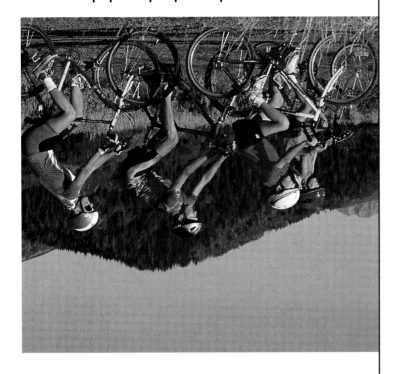

Flat tires can be fixed.
The boy pumps air into the tire.

There are many kinds of bikes.
Little children ride little bikes.

Then the bike is ready to go.
Ride safely!

This bike has two big wheels and two little training wheels.

Bikes have tires.
The tires go around the wheels.

Bikes have handlebars.

You hold on to the handlebars.
The handlebars help you steer.

You push down on the pedals.
The faster you pedal,
the faster the bike goes!

Bikes have seats.
Most bikes have one seat.

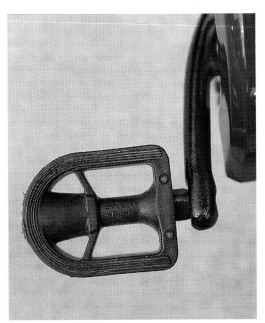

Bikes have pedals.

This bike has two seats.
Two people can ride on it.

These buildings are made
mostly of wood.

This building is small.
It has just
a few windows.

This is my favorite building.
I live here!

City Buildings

Christine Economos

City buildings come
in different sizes.

People work here.
is an office building.
This very tall tower

Take a look at a city.
You will see many buildings.

These buildings
are called brownstones.
People live here.

This red building is round.

This yellow building is shaped like a triangle.

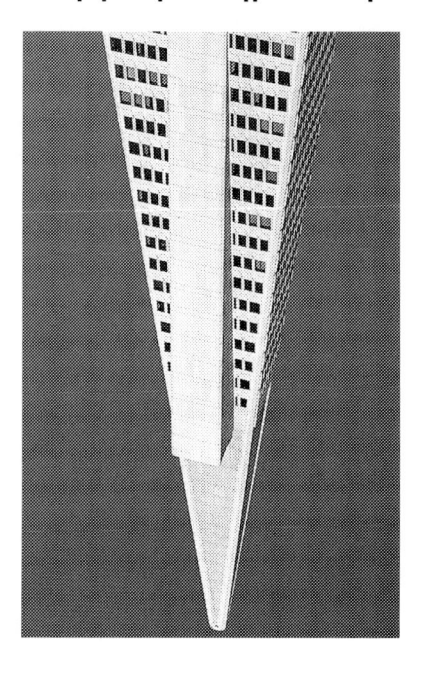

This building is made mostly of cement.

This building is big. It has many windows.

This building is made mostly of red brick.

City buildings come in many shapes. This building is low and wide.

This building is tall and thin.

City buildings can be made out of different things. This building is made mostly of glass and metal.

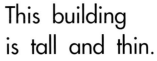

Sometimes you can see the moon during the day, too. But you will never see the sun at night.

Now the sun is high in the sky.

It is time to start a new day.

Day and Night

William Anton

the night is over.

The sun is rising.

It is time
to wake up!

When the sun rises again,

You can see the moon.
It looks thin for a few nights.

Now it is night.
You can see the stars.

Finally, it is a full moon.

It is noon.

You can see more and more of it.

Late in the afternoon
the sun is low in the sky.

Then, night after night,

Now the sun is setting.
It is evening.

in the air...

This bird can run.
Two long legs
help the bird run fast.

How many ways
can YOU move around?

How
Animals
Move

Brenda Parkes

This bird can fly.
Big wings help the bird
fly across the sea.

and on the ground.

This bee can fly.
Little wings help the bee
fly in and out of flowers.

People move
in many ways, too.

and swim.

climb...

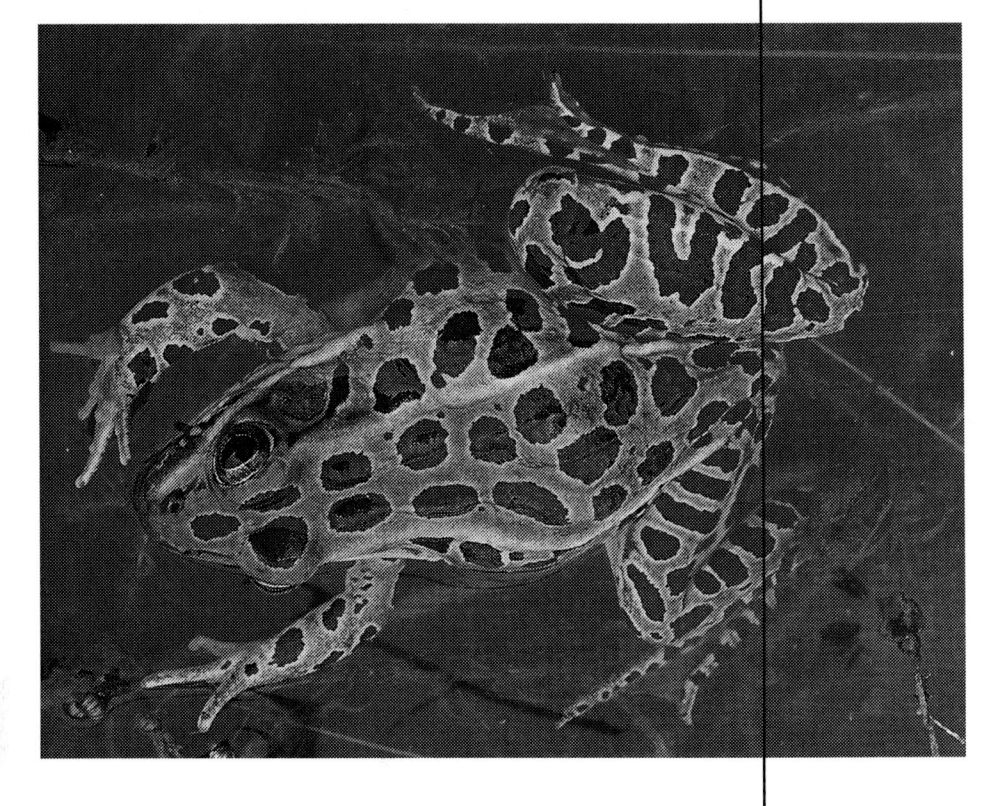

Animals move in so many ways.
They move in the water...

This leopard can run.
Four legs help it
run very fast.

This manatee uses its flippers
to swim in the sea.

This kangaroo can hop.
Strong back legs
help it hop a long way.

Who else can swim?
This fish uses its tail
and fins to swim.

This frog can hop.
Strong back legs
help a frog hop...

Their eyes are not open.
Their ears are not open.
They cannot walk.

Kittens

Brenda Parkes

Now the kittens are big enough for me to take one home.

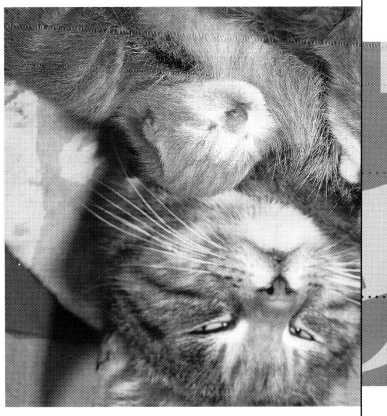

How Kittens Grow

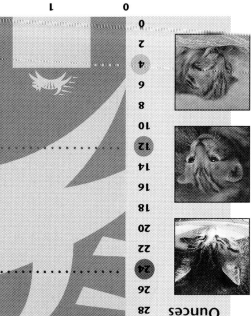

Weight in Ounces

0 2 4 6 8 10 12 14 16 18 20 22 24 26 28 30

The First Week

These kittens are
one day old.
They are very small.

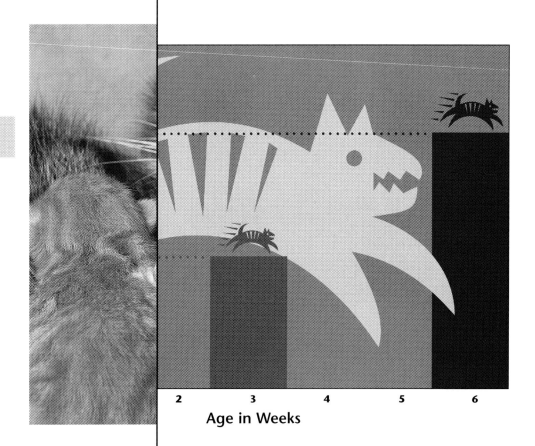

2   3   4   5   6

Age in Weeks

The mother cat feeds the kittens.
She cleans them
and keeps them warm.

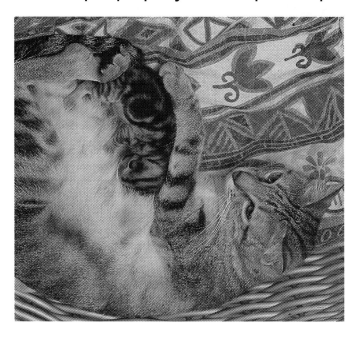

They are big enough
to explore their world.

Their eyes are open.
Their ears are open.
They can walk.

The mother cat still feeds
the kittens.
She still cleans them
and keeps them warm.

They can climb and jump.

The Third Week

These kittens are three weeks old. They are bigger.

The Sixth Week

When kittens are six weeks old they can eat by themselves.

Yes!

Christine Economos

Let's Make
Something New

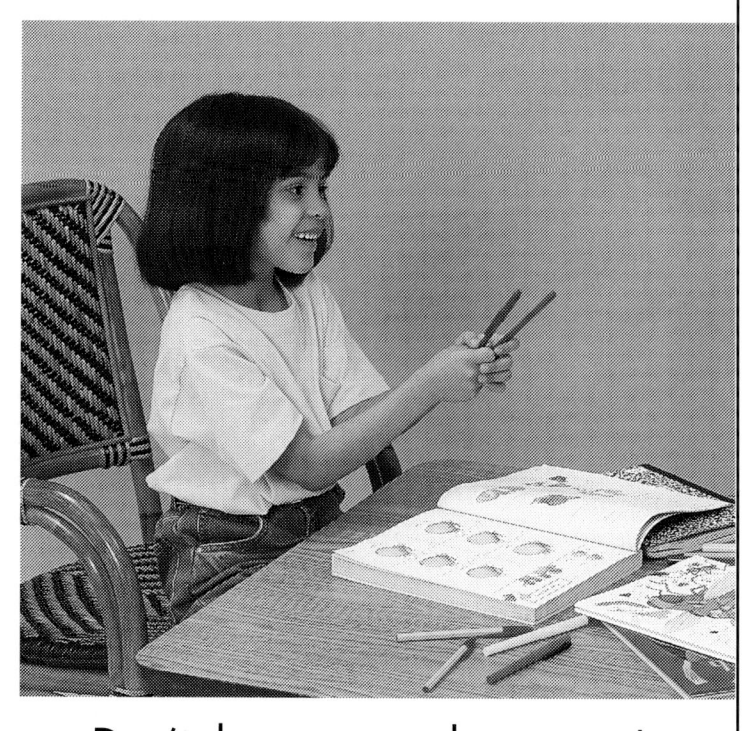

Don't throw away those pens!
We can use them.

Dad cuts a flap.
We push the flap in.

We are going to make
something new.

The bird feeder is ready.
We fill it with seeds.

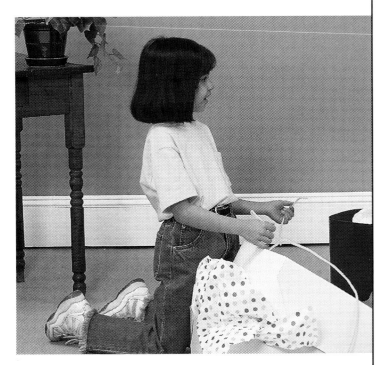

Don't throw out that string!
We can use it.

We hang it from a tree.
Will the birds come?

I put the string
through the holes.
We tie it.

Dad makes two holes
near the top of
the bottle.

We measure 2 inches
above the pens.

We are going to make
something new.

I push the pens
into the holes.

Don't throw out
that bottle!
We can use it.

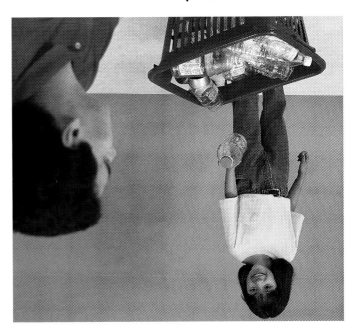

Dad makes two holes
near the bottom.

We are going to make
something for the birds.
It will look like this.

This rock looks like
a triangle.

You can find rocks in a river.

What do these rocks look like?

Rocks

Brenda Parkes

You can find rocks
on a mountain.

These rocks are tall and thin.
They look like statues.

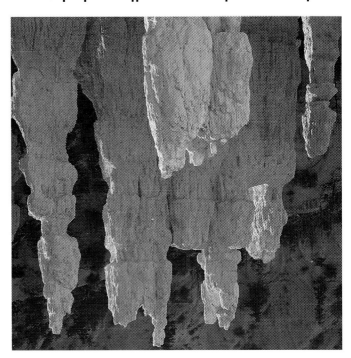

Rocks are everywhere.
You can find rocks on a beach.

These rocks are short and wide.
They look like blocks.

You can find rocks in a desert.

Rocks can be many shapes.
These rocks look like eggs.

People have even found rocks...

on the moon!

These rocks are small. Most grains of sand are rocks!

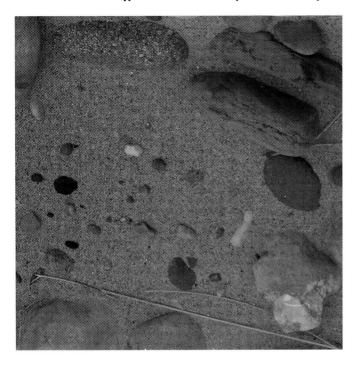

You can find rocks on a city street...

Rocks can be many sizes. This rock is big.

or in a garden.

The snail eats chalk, too.
The chalk makes its shell hard.

Our snails will live in boxes.
We need to make
good homes for them.

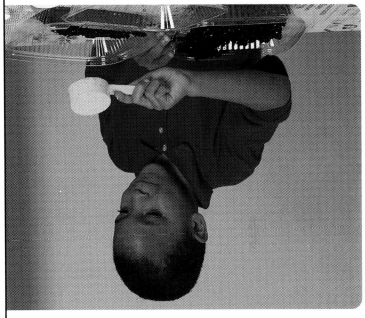

Friday

We know how
to take care of snails.
We can take our snails home!

Snails in School!

Christine Economos

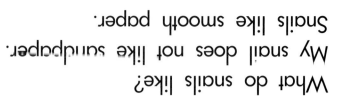

What do snails like?
My snail does not like sandpaper.
Snails like smooth paper.

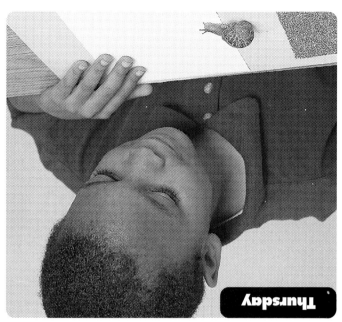

Thursday

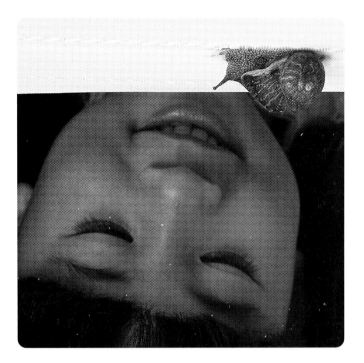

We will learn about them.
We can't wait!

Monday

Today the snails came.

My snail does not like
bright light.
Snails like cool, dark places.

We put in dirt.
We put in rocks.
We put in twigs.

The snail eats the lettuce.
Lettuce helps it grow.

I draw what I see.
I name the parts of my snail.

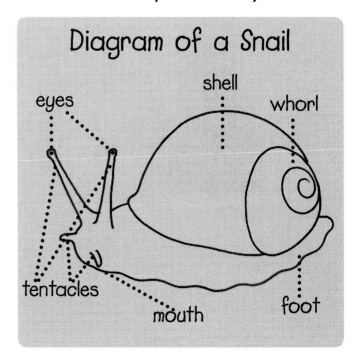

Diagram of a Snail

eyes
shell
whorl
tentacles
mouth
foot

I see four tentacles.
I see two tiny eyes.
I think the snail is looking at me!

The snail does not eat the lemon.

Will the snail come out?
I put a little water near it.
Nothing happens.

Tuesday

Wednesday

What do snails eat?
We will find out.

I blow on it gently.
A little head pops out.

Look at this thread.

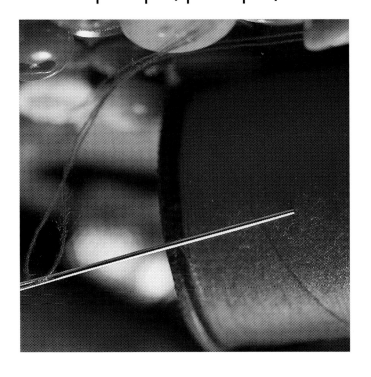

Do you know what this is?
Look closely.

It's a strawberry.
Yum!

Up Close

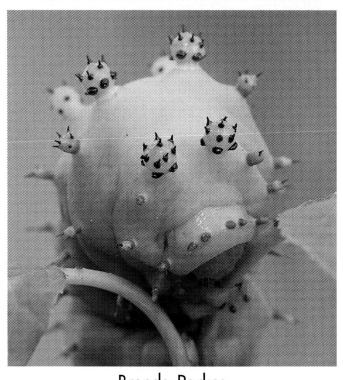

Brenda Parkes

It's a butterfly's wing.

Up close you will see that it is made up of many strands.

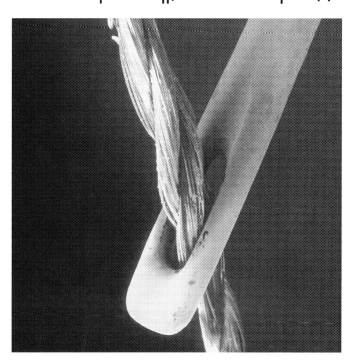

Do you know what this is?
Look closely.

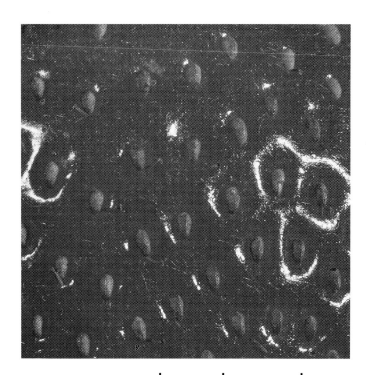

Here is something else up close.
Can you guess what this is?

It's a leaf.

Up close you will see that each grain of salt is a tiny cube.

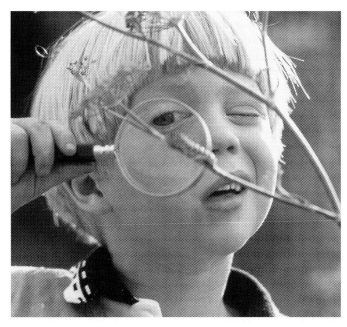

What is the boy looking through?
It's a magnifying glass.
It helps you look closely.

When you look closely,
you learn new things.
Look at this tree.

Look at this salt.

Do you know what this is?
Look closely.

It's a zebra.

Up close you will see why
its bark feels so rough.

People also change
from babies...

Some chicks will
become hens.

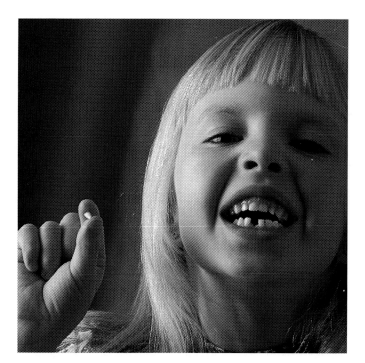

What change do you see here?

What Can Change?

Brenda Parkes

to adults.

Many things change.

to children…

These little chicks will grow and change.

This little spotted cub
will grow and change.

The sun will melt it.
Then the grass will grow.

They will become sunflowers.

Other things change.
How will this lake change
in the winter?

The water will freeze
and turn into ice.

Plants change, too.
These small plants will grow.

What will happen to this snow
in the spring?

It will become a big
golden mountain lion.

After many weeks, little plants can grow into big plants.

A garden needs plants.

What else does a garden need? Gardens need people, too.

What Does a Garden Need?

Judy Nayer

People use tools to dig up dirt.

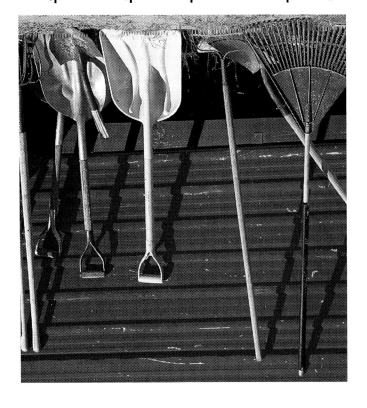

Different kinds of gardens grow in different places.

A garden needs dirt.

All gardens need
dirt, plants, sun, and water.

Some plants grow from seeds.

A garden needs time to grow.

A garden needs sun.
Some plants need lots of sun.

Other plants grow well
with just a little sun.

What if there is no rain?
People can water their gardens.

Other plants grow from bulbs.
People put the bulbs in the dirt.

A garden needs water.
Rain helps plants to grow.

These flowers grew from bulbs.

Parents take care of eggs
so babies hatch and grow.

Brenda Parkes

Where Are the Eggs?

Here they are.
They are in a nest in a tree.

This penguin will lay
her egg on the ice.

Where will this robin
lay her eggs?

Where is the egg now?
The father penguin has it
on his feet.

Some animals lay eggs.
They lay their eggs
in many different places.

He keeps the egg warm until
it hatches into a baby penguin.

Where will this sea turtle lay her eggs?

Here they are. They are in a nest on the ground, too.

They are under a leaf. When the babies hatch, they will eat the leaf.

Where will this goose lay her eggs?

Where will this butterfly
lay her eggs?

Here they are.
They are in a nest
on the ground.

Here they are.
They are in a hole
in the sand.

Where will this alligator
lay her eggs?

Weaverbirds can build.
They build nests.

Animals build to make a safe
place to sleep, raise their babies,
or keep their food.

Animals Build

Adrienne Betz

The lodges are made
of sticks and mud.

Spiders can build, too.
They weave sticky webs.

Beavers can build.
They build lodges.

These webs are traps!
Spiders use webs to catch food.

Bees can build.
Worker bees make wax.
They use the wax to build little cells.

The cells make up
big hives.

Bats can build.
They chew leaves
to build tents to sleep in.

The nests are made
of grass and twigs.

Many tiny insects work together
to build the mounds.

Chimpanzees can build.
They build beds in the treetops.

Termites can build.
They build tall mounds.

They build their beds
from branches, leaves, and twigs.

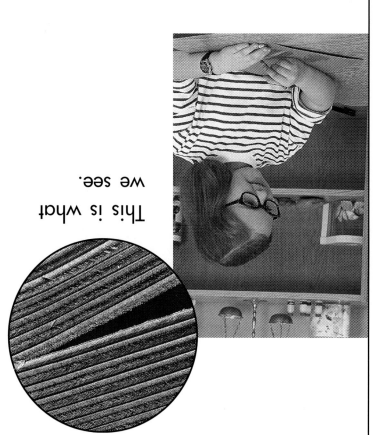

This is what we see.

What will we find out about these shells? We can sort them.

• At the Science Center

Brenda Parkes

What will we find out next?

What will we find out today?

I can use it to look at a honeybee's leg.

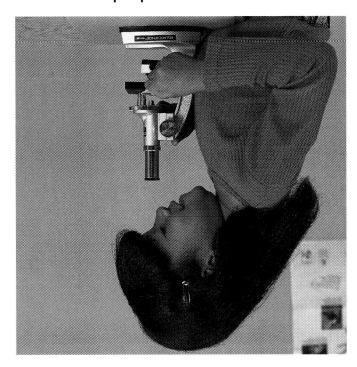

We will work in the science center.

antenna
head
thorax
wing
eye
leg
abdomen

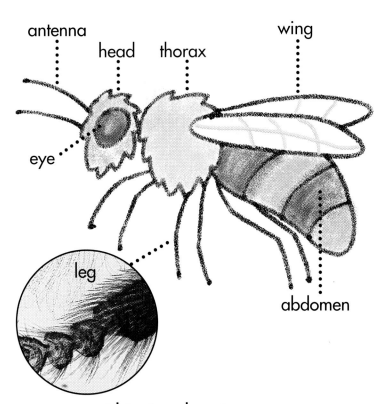

This is what I see.

They are different shapes.
They are different sizes.

What can we see with
a microscope?
We can use it to look at a feather.

What will we find out
about this water?
We can measure the water.

One cup of water is in each container.
The water takes the shape
of the containers.

I draw what we saw.
I write about what we found out.

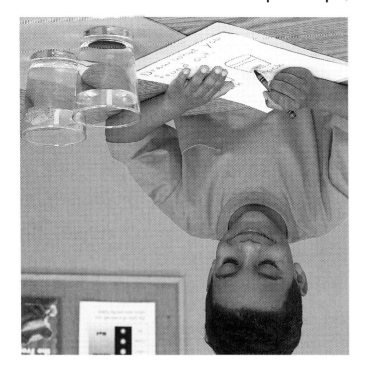

I can weigh them.
Will these five small shells
weigh the same as this big shell?

Some things can float in water.
Can the cork float?
Can the rock float?

I draw what I saw.
I write about what
I found out.

The animals of the coral reef are amazing.
What will the diver photograph next on the coral reef?

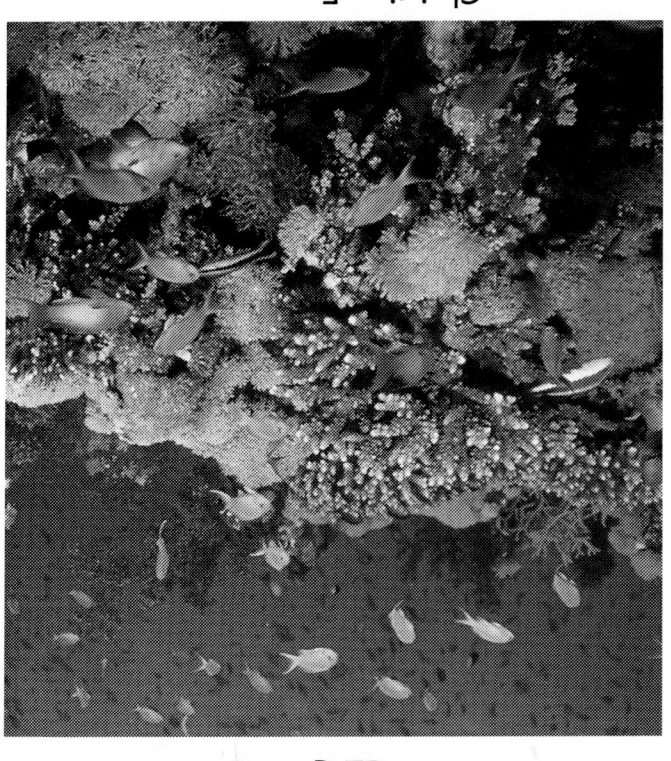

The Coral Reef

Christine Economos

A blue tang fish lives here.
The baby blue tang fish
is yellow.

The black dots are the clam's eyes.
Its many eyes help the clam
see danger.

Many other sea animals
live in the coral reef, too.

A puffer fish lives here.
What happens when it
is in danger?

This is a coral reef.
It is made up of tiny animals
called corals.

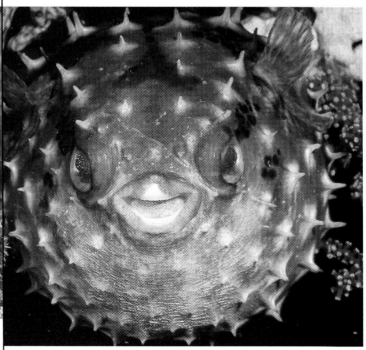

It puffs itself up.
Then it looks scary.

A big blue clam lives here.
Can you see the black dots?

As it grows, it changes color.
It turns blue.

A green lettuce slug lives here.
How did this animal get its name?

It looks like lettuce, but it doesn't taste like it!

These circles help the octopus taste and feel.

Orange and white clownfish live here. They stay near an animal with green tentacles. Can you see the green tentacles?

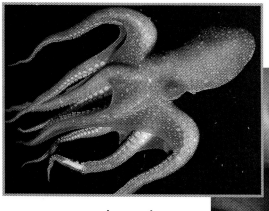

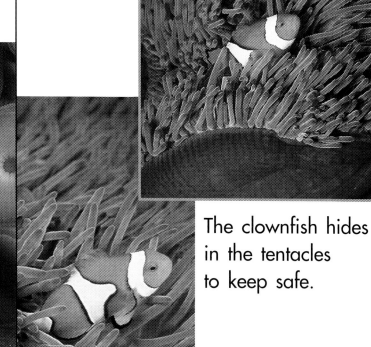

An octopus lives here. Can you see the many circles on its eight long arms?

The clownfish hides in the tentacles to keep safe.

Some dried corn will be used by factories to make different foods.

Farms use machines to plant corn. This machine plants the seeds and covers them with soil.

Corn is good to eat. Do you eat breakfast food made from corn?

Corn: From Farm to Table

William Anton

Foods Made From Corn

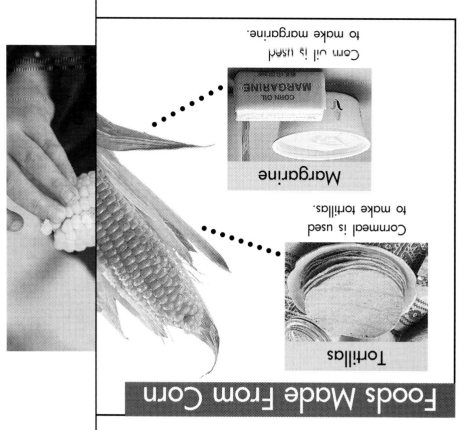

Tortillas
Cornmeal is used to make tortillas.

Margarine
Corn oil is used to make margarine.

Farms grow corn for people and animals to eat.

Corn is good to eat.
You can eat corn like this.

Jelly beans
Corn syrup is used to make jelly beans.

Popcorn
Dried corn is used to make popcorn.

This elevator loads
dried corn into silos.

Soon the plants begin to grow.

Now the corn is ripe.

Farms use machines to pick the corn.
This machine picks ears of corn
right off the stalks.

This truck is loaded with dried corn.

Corn plants need water to grow tall.

This tractor takes ears of corn
to the market.

Farms use machines to water corn.
This machine sprays water
on the corn.

We use electricity in many ways.
We use electricity to
light our homes.

How do we use wood?
Wood can be used to build houses.

make this car go fast!
Electricity, wood, and oil
help us in many ways.

From the Earth

William Anton

We get wood from trees.
Wood can be used in many ways.

We use electricity to run machines.

Wood

Every day we use things
that come from the Earth.
There are trees on the Earth.

Some machines run on
electric batteries.
These little batteries
can...

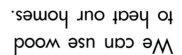

We can use wood to heat our homes.

Power lines carry the electricity from the power plants and dams. The power lines bring electricity to our homes.

How do we use oil?
We can use oil
to heat our homes.

We can use oil to run our cars.

Dams use water to help make electricity.

Oil

There is oil deep in the Earth. People use big machines to drill for the oil.

Electricity

Some oil goes to power plants. Power plants use the oil or coal to make electricity.

They use machines to pump the oil out. Oil can be used in many ways.

The scales help
the snake climb.

The polar bear is
a good swimmer.

Think of the animals you know.
Which have fur or feathers?
Which have scales or skin?

Fur, Feathers, Scales, Skin

Christine Economos

The fur keeps the bear warm.

Skin

Many animals have skin.
Elephants have thick skin.

Fur

Many animals have fur.
This polar bear
has thick fur.

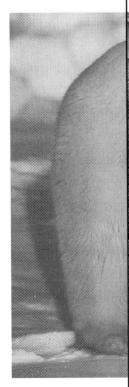

Elephants eat leaves from trees.
The thick skin keeps them
from getting cut and scratched.

When it gets back on land
water drips from its fur.
It shakes itself to dry its fur.

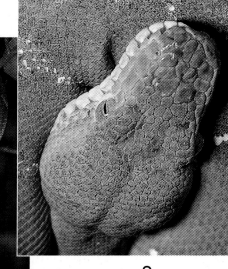

This snake has
smooth green scales.

Pheasants have feathers.
This pheasant lives on
the ground.

The pheasant's feathers are the same
color as the grass.
This helps the pheasant hide.

The scales help it to keep cool
in the hot desert sun.

Feathers

Many animals have feathers.
This parrot has different
kinds of feathers.

Scales

Many animals have scales.
This lizard has scales.
The lizard's scales
are brown and rough.

One kind is little and soft.
Another kind is long and smooth.
The long feathers help the parrot fly.

The last thing
we add is the nuts.

Banana Bread

Here is what
we need to make
banana bread.

We measured and stirred.
We waited for the bread to bake.
Now we will eat banana bread!

Let's Bake

Christine Economos

The heat inside the oven
will change the batter.
It will change from sticky batter
into bread.

These bananas are very ripe.
Grandma says they are
still good to eat.

She says we can use them
to make banana bread.

We pour the batter into the pan.
Now the bread will bake.

3 ripe bananas
2 eggs
2 cups flour
3/4 cup sugar
1 teaspoon salt
1 teaspoon baking powder
1/2 cup chopped walnuts

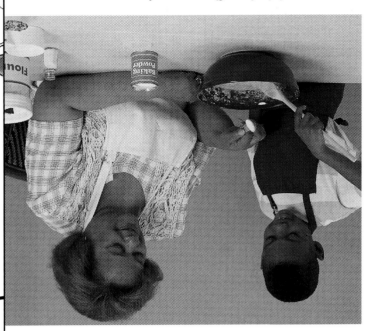

We add the flour, salt,
and baking powder.
Next we add the sugar and stir.

We need other tools, too.
We will use a big bowl for mixing.
We will use a fork for mashing.

We will use a big spoon for stirring.
We will use a pan for baking.

Grandma cracks the eggs
into the bowl.
Then I mix it all together.

We also need cups and spoons
like these.

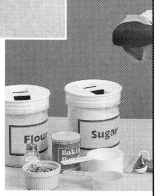

We are ready to start.
I mash the bananas
with the fork.

"You need to measure everything
just right," Grandma says.

This boy's shadow is not flat.
His shadow bends
because the steps bend.

We can get light
from electric lamps.

How does your shadow change?

Light and Shadow

William Anton

We get light from the sun.

Even a small thing can have a big shadow!

Light is all around us.

The boy and his bat
block out the light.
Can you see his shadow?

This girl's body blocks out the light.
You can see her shadow
on the ground.

This girl's shadow is flat.
Her shadow is flat
because the ground is flat.

We can get light from flashlights.
We need light to see.

A shadow is dark.
A shadow has a shape.

Light can shine through some things.
The sun shines through these windows.

When something blocks out the light
you can see its shadow.

These curtains only let
some light through.

When I brush my teeth
I taste and smell the toothpaste.
I can also see myself in the mirror.

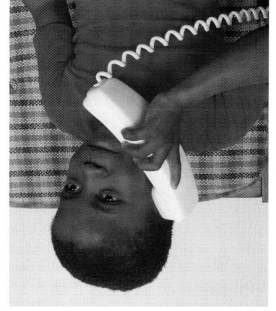

I use my ears to hear.
I can hear many things.

I use my senses in many ways.
How will you use your senses today?

Our Senses

Adrienne Betz

When I go to the beach
I hear sounds with a shell.
I feel the wet sand
and cool water.

I see colorful pictures.
What will you see today?

I see my friends playing.

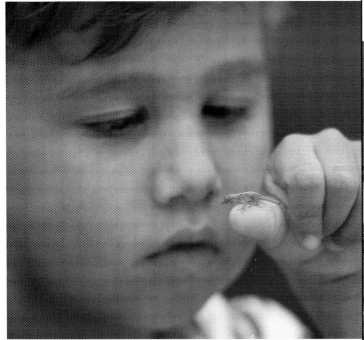

I use my eyes to see.
I can see many things.

I hear my friends cheering.
What will you hear today?

When I play I hear my music.
I use other senses, too.
I feel and see the guitar.

I use my fingers and my skin to feel.
I can feel many things.

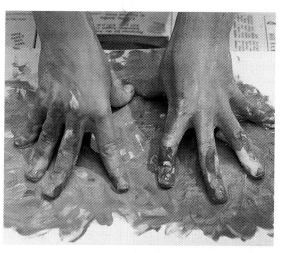

I feel wet sticky paint.
What will you feel today?

I can taste something sour!
What will you taste today?

I use my nose to smell.
I can smell many things.

I use my tongue to taste.
I can taste something sweet.

I smell fresh bread.
What will you smell today?

Brenda Parkes

Recycle It!

Look what I made!
You can recycle, too.

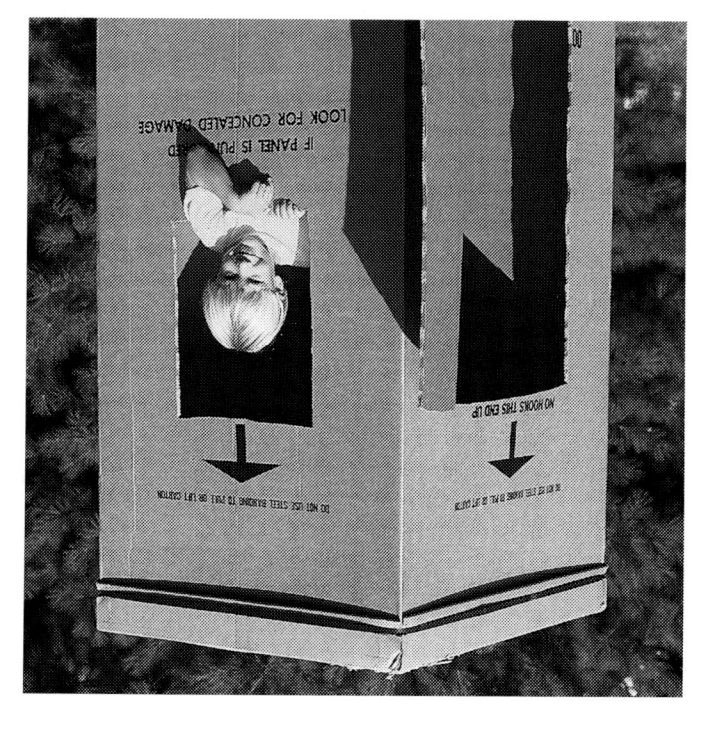

People recycle paper…

Old cans can be
used to make
new things.
This house is made
of cement
and recycled cans!

They can be recycled.
Every week the recycling truck
comes to our street.

You can recycle in the classroom.
Old bottles can be used
to make pretty vases.

Many of the things people throw
away can be used again.

You can recycle on the playground.
How were old tires used here?

These children are making new paper from old paper.

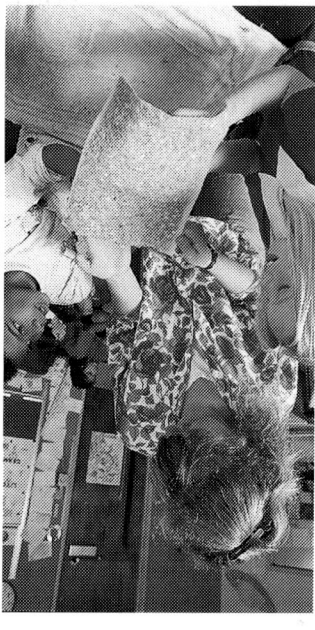

Paper is recycled.

and plastic.

This slide is made from recycled plastic, too.

People recycle glass...

Plastic is recycled.
These pails are made from recycled plastic.

and cans.

or play a violin.
What other ways
do people make music?

We can use our voices
to talk and laugh.

or that a parade is coming!
What sounds can you make?

Sounds All Around

Angela Shelf Medearis

We can use our voices
to cheer.

Sounds can tell you that it is time
to wake up...

We can make many sounds.
We can whisper.

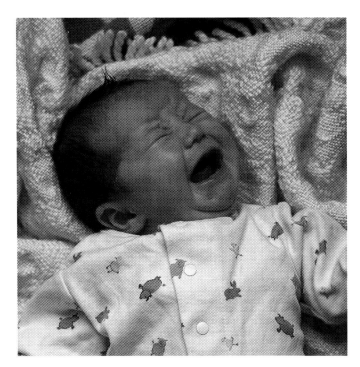

that the baby wants to eat...

We can use our voices to sing
and make music.

Music is made up of sounds.
People make music when they
blow into a trumpet...

Weather makes sounds.
The wind whooshes
through the trees and grass.

Lightning cracks and thunder booms.
What other sounds
does weather make?

This drill goes rat-a-tat-tat.
What other sounds
do machines make?

Many animals make sounds.
Some animals make loud sounds.
Lions roar.

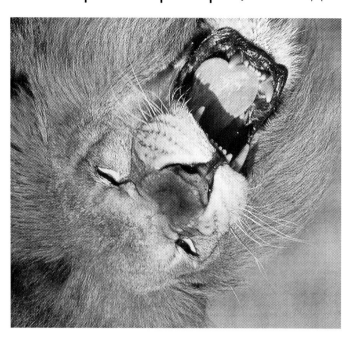

Machines make sounds.
Trains chug and clatter
along the tracks.

Baby ducks quack.
What other sounds
do animals make?

There are bright stars
on the Hunter's knee and his sword.
There is a bright star on his shoulder.

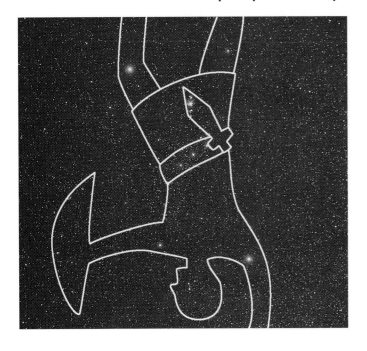

Stars look little because
they are so far away.

We see this yellow star during the day.
It is our sun!

Stars

Christine Economos

There are so many
you cannot count them.

Find the brightest star
in this photo.
It is part of a star picture
named the Big Dog.

The bright star is called the dog star.
It is the brightest star in the sky.

At night you can see stars.

This is a cluster of stars.
It is called the Seven Sisters.

Sometimes you can see stars
in a group.
These groups are called clusters.

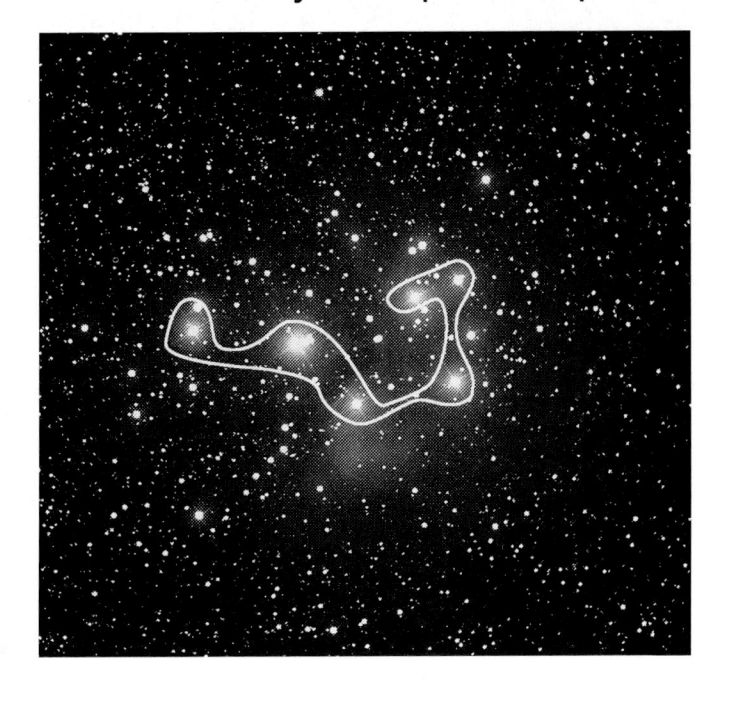

Some star pictures look like people.
This is called the Hunter.
There are three stars on his belt.

Stars are really giant
balls of very hot gas.
They glow because
they are so hot.

The color of a star tells you which stars are the hottest.

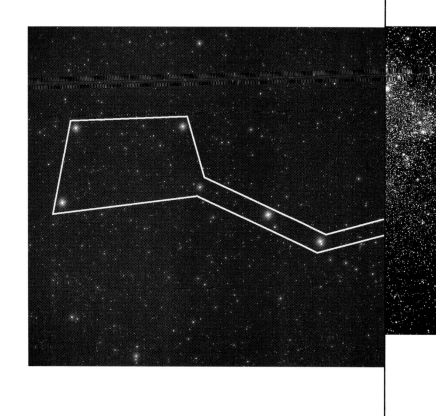

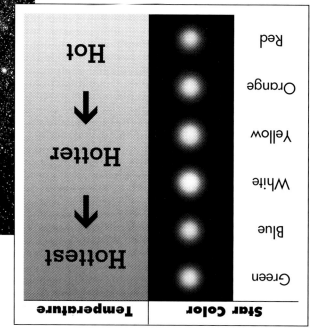

Temperature	Star Color
Hot ↓ Hotter ↓ Hottest	Red
	Orange
	Yellow
	White
	Blue
	Green

What color stars do you see here?
How hot are they?

Some stars seem to make
a picture in the sky.
Long ago people named
these pictures.
This is the Big Dipper.

Taking Care of Baby

Baby turtles
take care of themselves.
They crawl to the sea
and swim away.

Kangaroos

Who takes care of this baby?

Elephants travel in herds.
All the bigger elephants
help take care of this baby.

Its mother takes care
of this baby.
She made this den to keep
her babies safe and warm.

Look at this baby!

Sea Turtles

Foxes

Who takes care of this baby?

It has just hatched from its egg.
Who will take care of this baby turtle?

Its mother takes care of this baby.
She carries the baby in her pouch.

Who takes care of this baby?

Elephants

Lions

Who takes care of
these babies?

Two mothers team up.
They help each other take care
of their cubs.

A babysitter takes care of these babies. The sitter watches them while their parents search for food.

Who takes care of this baby?

Robins

Meerkats

Who takes care of this baby?

Both its mother and father take care of this baby. They bring it food.

It is getting warmer.
The temperature is 60°F.

Now it is even cooler.
The pumpkins are ready to pick.

Weather Temperatures

Fall		Winter		Spring		Summer

We watched the weather.
The temperature changes
through the seasons.

Watching the Weather

Marcia Freeman

It is getting cool.
The temperature is 60°F.

We are watching the weather.
It is sunny and very hot.

Summer Weather

Fall Weather

We are watching the weather.
The leaves are changing colors.

The temperature is 80° F.
We can cool off in the sprinkler!

Leaves are falling from the trees.
The temperature is 50°F.

The flowers begin to bloom
and grow tall.

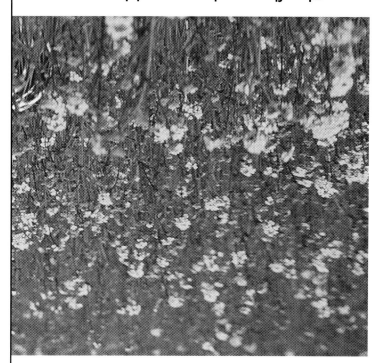

Now it is not so cold.
We can see the ground.

The snow is melting.
The temperature is 40°F.

The trees begin to get new leaves.
The temperature is 50°F.

We are watching the weather.
It is cold.
We can see ice and snow.

Winter Weather

Spring Weather

We are watching the weather.
It is raining.

We are making a snowman.
The temperature is just 20°F.

We draw pictures.

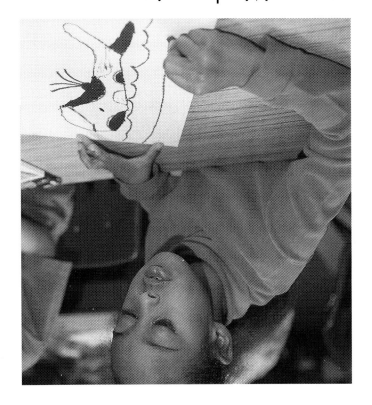

Scientists measure…

We are scientists every day.

What Do Scientists Do?

Daniel Jacobs

and listen.

Scientists look…

We ask questions and work together to find out answers.

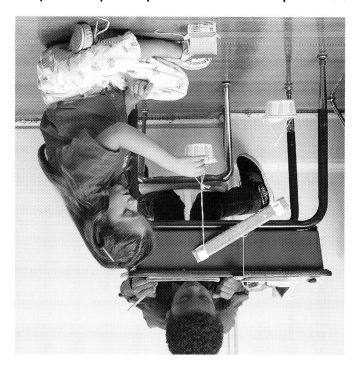

We make charts to show what we find.

and take notes.

We watch how things change.

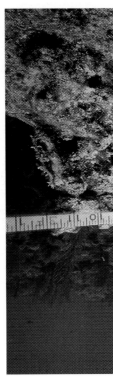

They also make charts
to show what they found.

We are scientists, too.
We look at things.

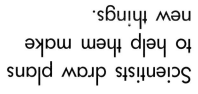

Scientists draw plans to help them make new things.

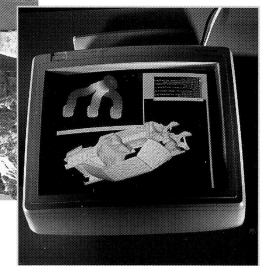

and take notes.

Scientists take photographs to show what they found.

We measure…

When it is warm,
it can fall as rain.

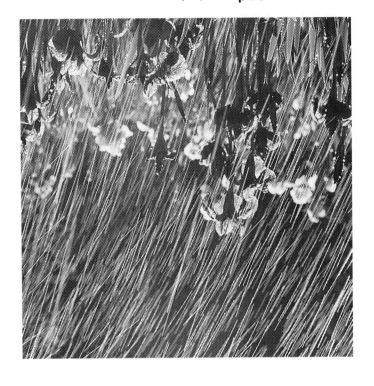

Index

Where Does the Water Go?

William Anton

It is raining! The rain has made lots of puddles.

The Water Cycle

Clouds form.

Clouds get bigger.

Water turns into vapor and goes into the air.

Clouds get bigger and bigger.

Rain falls.

Water is amazing!

Puddles are fun to jump in,
but puddles dry up.
When puddles dry up, tiny
drops called water vapor
go into the air.

Water vapor changes
back into water.
When it is cold,
it can fall as snow.

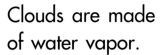

Clouds are made
of water vapor.

As the air soaks up more and more water,
the clouds get bigger and bigger.

Sometimes you can see water vapor in the air. The mist on this lake is water vapor.

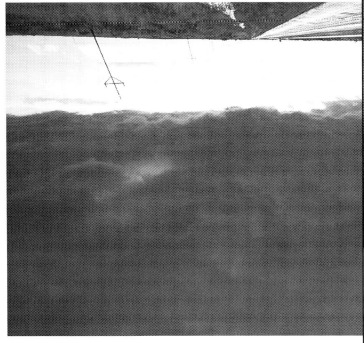

What will happen?

The steam rising from this kettle is water vapor.

These big dark clouds are full of water vapor now.

Discovery Links Photo Credits

Set A

Animals From Long Ago:
Cover: Neg. No. 5492(3), Courtesy Dept. of Library Services, American Museum of Natural History, NY; Page 2: Neg. No. K17197, Photo by Denis Finnin, Courtesy Dept. of Library Services, American Museum of Natural History, NY; Page 3: Neg. No. 54111(3), Courtesy Dept. of Library Services, American Museum of Natural History, NY; Pages 4–5: Neg. No. 5187(2), Photo by Denis Finnin, Courtesy Dept. of Library Services, American Museum of Natural History, NY; Page 6: Neg. No. 4949(2), Photo by Denis Finnin, Courtesy Dept. of Library Services, American Museum of Natural History, NY; Page 7: Stephen J. Krasemann/Photo Researchers, Inc.; Pages 8–9: Neg. No. 35112, Photo by A. E. Anderson, Courtesy Dept. of Library Services, American Museum of Natural History, NY; Page 10: Neg No. 5798(2), Photo by Denis Finnin, Courtesy Dept. of Library Services, American Museum of Natural History, NY; Page 11: George Holton/Photo Researchers, Inc.; Pages 12–13: Neg. No. 5493(2), Courtesy Dept. of Library Services, American Museum of Natural History, NY; Pages 14–15: Gregory S. Paul; Page 15: Leonard Lee Rue III/Photo Researchers, Inc.; Page 16: Michael Collier

Animal Messengers:
Cover: Hans Reinhard/Bruce Coleman, Inc.; Page 2: Myrleen Ferguson/PhotoEdit; Page 3: David Young-Wolff/PhotoEdit; Page 4: ©1998 PhotoDisk, Inc.; Page 5: Elaine Rebman/Photo Researchers, Inc.; Page 6: Daniel J. Cox/Natural Exposures; Pages 6–7: Jeff Foott/Bruce Coleman, Inc.; Pages 8–9: Peter Skinner/Photo Researchers, Inc.; Page 9: Stephen J. Krasemann/DRK Photo; Pages 10–11: Hans Pfleschinger/Peter Arnold, Inc.; Page 11: D. Thompson/Animals Animals; Page 12: Kennan Ward/Bruce Coleman, Inc.; Pages 12–13: Renee Lynn/Photo Researchers, Inc.; Page 14: Roy Morsch/The Stock Market; Page 15: Roy Morsch/The Stock Market

At the Playground:
Cover: Phyllis Picardi/The Picture Cube; Page 2: Chip Henderson/Tony Stone Images; Page 3: Lawrence Migdale/Stock Boston; Page 4: June Bug Clark/Photo Researchers, Inc.; Page 5: Jim Cummins/FPG International; Page 6: Jeff Isaac Greenberg/Photo Researchers, Inc.; Page 7: SuperStock; Page 8: David Young-Wolff/PhotoEdit; Page 9: Ralph A. Reinhold/The Picture Cube; Page 10: David Young-Wolff/PhotoEdit; Page 11: J. Taposchaner/FPG International; Page 12: Photo Works/Photo Researchers, Inc.; Page 13: Crews/Image Works; Page 14: (left) Martin Rogers/Tony Stone Images, (right) Michael Hart/FPG International; Page 15: Arthur Tilley/FPG International; Page 16: Spencer Grant/PhotoEdit

Beaks:
Cover: Stuart Westmorland/Tony Stone Images; Page 2: Momatiuk & Eastcott/Photo Researchers, Inc.; Page 3: C. Allan Morgan/Peter Arnold, Inc.; Page 4: Steve Kaufman/DRK Photo; Page 5: Partridge OSF/Animals Animals; Page 6: William H. Mullins/Photo Researchers, Inc.; Page 7: Alan D. Carey/Photo Researchers, Inc.; Page 8: Nora & Rick Bowers/The Wildlife Collection; Page 9: Joe McDonald/Tom Stack & Associates; Page 10: Jeff Lepore/Photo Researchers, Inc.; Page 11: Zig Leszczynski/Animals Animals; Page 12: Leonard Lee Rue/Animals Animals; Page 13: T.A. Wiewandt/DRK Photo; Page 14: Courtney Milne/Masterfile; Page 15: Luiz C. Marigo/Peter Arnold, Inc.; Page 16: Ralph A. Reinhold/Animals Animals

Bikes:
Cover: Jon Feingersh/The Stock Market; Page 2: Bob Daemmrich/Stock Boston; Pages 2–3: Lori Adamski Peek/Tony Stone Images; Page 4: David Young-Wolff/PhotoEdit; Page 5: Myrleen Ferguson/PhotoEdit; Pages 6–7: Alan Schein/The Stock Market; Page 7: Jonathan Nourok/PhotoEdit; Page 8: The Image Bank; Page 9: Myrleen Cate/Tony Stone Images; Page 10: David Young-Wolff/PhotoEdit; Pages 10–11: Larry Brownstein/Rainbow; Page 12: Grant Faint/The Image Bank; Page 13: Dana White/PhotoEdit; Page 14: Dana White/PhotoEdit; Page 15: Dana White/PhotoEdit; Page 16: Aaron Haupt/Photo Researchers, Inc.

City Buildings:
Cover: Vic Bider/PhotoEdit; Page 2: Sue Pashko/Envision; Page 3: James Blank/The Stock Market; Page 4: Peter Vadnai/The Stock Market; Pages 4–5: Alan Schein/The Stock Market; Pages 6–7: Alan Schein/The Stock Market; Page 7: Alan Schein/The Stock Market; Page 8: Berenholtz/The Stock Market; Pages 8–9: Jeff Greenberg/Leo De Wys, Inc.; Page 10: Jeff Greenberg/Rainbow; Page 11: Everett C. Johnson/Leo De Wys, Inc.; Page 12: Coco McCoy/Rainbow; Page 13: Lawrence Migdale/Photo Researchers, Inc.; Page 14: Cosmo Condina/Tony Stone Images; Pages 14–15: Norman O. Tomalin/Bruce Coleman, Inc.; Page 16: Tony Freeman/PhotoEdit

Day and Night:
Cover: SuperStock; Page 2: Lynn M. Stone/The Picture Cube; Page 3: Richard Hutchings/Photo Researchers, Inc.; Page 4: Stephanie Rausser/FPG International; Page 5: Ken Lax/Photo Researchers, Inc.; Page 6: Lawrence Migdale/Photo Researchers, Inc.; Page 7: SuperStock; Page 8: Frank Zullo/Photo Researchers, Inc.; Page 9: J. MacPherson/The Stock Market; Page 10: Toni Angermayer/Photo Researchers, Inc.; Page 11: R. B. Sanchez/The Stock Market; Page 12: Bill Bachman/Photo Researchers, Inc.; Page 13: Jeff Lepore/

Set B

Animals Build:
Cover: Gerard Lacz/Animals Animals; Page 2: Robert Lankinen/The Wildlife Collection; Page 3: C. C. Lockwood/DRK Photo; Page 4: (left) M.P. Kahl/DRK Photo, (right) M.P. Kahl/DRK Photo; Page 5: Stanley Breeden/DRK Photo; Page 6: Jack Swenson/The Wildlife Collection; Page 7: S. Morris/Animals Animals; Pages 8–9: Norman Lightfoot/Photo Researchers, Inc.; Page 9: Robert & Linda Mitchell Photography; Pages 10–11: Baron Hugo Van Lawick/The National Geographic Society; Page 12: Gilbert S. Grant/Photo Researchers, Inc.; Pages 12–13: Gilbert S. Grant/Photo Researchers, Inc.; Pages 14–15: Larry Ulrich/DRK Photo; Page 16: Tom & Pat Leeson/DRK Photo

At the Science Center:
Page 13: (top) Jerome Wexler/Photo Researchers, Inc.; Page 15: Gary Retherford/Photo Researchers, Inc., illustration by Debrah Welling and Ginidir Marshall; All other photographs: Stephen Ogilvy

The Coral Reef:
Cover: Norbert Wu Photography; Pages 2–3: Fred Bavendam/Peter Arnold, Inc.; Page 4: Larry Lipsky/Bruce Coleman, Inc.; Page 5: Larry Lipsky/Bruce Coleman, Inc.; Page 6: Norbert Wu Photography; Page 7: Norbert Wu Photography; Pages 8–9: Doug Perrine/DRK Photo; Page 10: Norbert Wu/DRK Photo; Pages 10–11: Randy Morse/Tom Stack & Associates; Pages 12–13: Pete Atkinson/Masterfile; Page 14: Jane Burton/Bruce Coleman, Inc.; Pages 14–15: Norbert Wu Photography; Page 16: Norbert Wu Photography

Corn: From Farm to Table:
Cover: Gary Holscher/Tony Stone Images; Pages 2–3: Sara Gray/Tony Stone Images; Page 3: Rick Miller/AG Stock USA; Pages 4–5: Grant Heilman/Grant Heilman Photography; Page 5: PhotoEdit; Page 6: Lance Nelson/The Stock Market; Page 7: SuperStock; Page 8: Mark Gibson/AG Stock USA; Pages 8–9: Bill Stormont/The Stock Market; Page 10: Lowell J. Georgia/Photo Researchers, Inc.; Page 11: Peter Beck/The Stock Market; Page 12: N. Warren Winter/AG Stock USA; Pages 12–13: Robert Frerck/Woodfin Camp & Associates; Pages 14–15: (top left) David Young-Wolff/PhotoEdit, (bottom left) Michael Newman/PhotoEdit, (center) Laszlo Studio/The Stock Market, (top right) Charles Krebs/The Stock Market, (bottom right) David Young-Wolff/PhotoEdit; Page 16: Steven Gottlieb/FPG International

From the Earth:
Cover: Tom Bean/Tony Stone Images; Page 2: David R. Frazier Photography; Page 3: Bruce M. Wellman/Stock Boston; Pages 4–5: Mark Joseph/Tony Stone Images; Page 5: Kevin Syms/David R. Frazier Photography; Page 6: George Hunter/Tony Stone Images; Page 7: Patrick Rouillard/The Stock Market; Page 8: Chris Hackett/The Image Bank;

Pages 8–9: Jonathan Novrol/PhotoEdit; Page 10: Chromosohm/Photo Researchers, Inc.; Page 11: Index Stock Photography, Inc.; Page 12: A. Ramey/PhotoEdit; Page 13: Warren Morgan/Westlight; Pages 14–15: HMS Images/The Image Bank; Page 15: David R. Frazier Photography; Page 16: David R. Frazier Photography

Fur, Feathers, Scales, Skin:
Cover: John Shaw/Tom Stack & Associates; Pages 2–3: Norbert Rosing/Animals Animals; Page 4: Gerard Lacz/Animals Animals; Pages 4–5: Tom & Pat Leeson/DRK Photo; Pages 6–7: Kevin Schafer; Page 8: Wendy Shattil & Bob Rozinski/Tom Stack & Associates; Pages 8–9: Tom & Pat Leeson/DRK Photo; Pages 10–11: Michael H. Francis/The Wildlife Collection; Page 12: Michael Fogden/DRK Photo; Pages 12–13: Gerry Ellis/ENP Images; Pages 14–15: Carl Purcell/Photo Researchers, Inc.; Page 16: Tom & Dee Ann McCarthy/The Stock Market

Let's Bake:
All photographs: Stephen Ogilvy

Light and Shadow:
Cover: Frank Siteman/The Picture Cube; Pages 2–3: Frank Orel/Tony Stone Images; Page 4: Dale Guldan/The Picture Cube; Page 5: David Woods/The Stock Market; Pages 6–7: Jerome Wexler/FPG International; Page 7: Frank Siteman/The Picture Cube; Page 8: Margaret Miller/Photo Researchers, Inc.; Page 9: Charles Blecker/The Picture Cube; Page 10: Alan Oddie/PhotoEdit; Page 11: Curtis Ryan Lew/International Stock; Page 12: Jerry Koontz/The Picture Cube; Page 13: Neil Ricklen/PhotoEdit; Pages 14–15: Chris Rogers/Rainbow; Page 16: Barry Hennings/Photo Researchers, Inc.

Our Senses:
Cover: Myleen Ferguson/PhotoEdit; Page 2: Frank Simonetti/The Picture Cube; Page 3: Photo Works/Monkmeyer Press Photos; Page 4: Michal Heron/Monkmeyer Press Photos; Page 5: Michael Newman/PhotoEdit; Page 6: Peter Steiner/The Stock Market; Page 7: Dan McCoy/Rainbow; Page 8: Arthur Tilley/FPG International; Page 9: Maggie Leonard/Rainbow; Page 10: David Young-Wolff/PhotoEdit; Page 11: Myrlen Cate/Tony Stone Images; Page 12: Charles Gupton/The Stock Market; Page 13: Jalandoni/Monkmeyer Press Photos; Page 14: Willie L. Hill, Jr./Stock Boston; Page 15: Ariel Skelley/The Stock Market; Page 16: Lawrence Migdale

Recycle It!:
Cover: David Sailors/The Stock Market; Page 2: Jon Feingersh/The Stock Market; Page 3: David R. Frazier/Photo Researchers, Inc.; Page 4: Jose L. Pelaez/The Stock Market; Page 5: Bill Truslow/Tony Stone Images; Page 6: David Young-Wolff/PhotoEdit; Page 7: Jim Corwin/Tony Stone Images; Page 8: Renee Lynn/Photo Researchers, Inc.; Page 9: Renee Lynn/Photo Researchers, Inc. (left), Renee Lynn/Photo Researchers, Inc. (right); Page 10: David Pollack/The Stock Market; Page 11: Tony Freeman/